You Make the Decision

Fifteen Topics for Critical Thinking

James M. Vardaman

TSURUMI SHOTEN

You Make the Decision
Fifteen Topics for Critical Thinking

by James M. Vardaman

Copyright ©2015 by James Vardaman

All rights reserved.
No part of this book may be used or reproduced without the written permission of the publisher.

Photo Credits

page

    5 © oticki—Fotolia.com
    9 © ag visuell—Fotolia.com
   13 © 7maru—Fotolia.com
   21 © Tom Wang—Fotolia.com
   25 © adam121—Fotolia.com
   29 © Piotr Adamowicz—Fotolia.com
   33 © alphaspirit—Fotolia.com
   41 © paylessimages—Fotolia.com
   45 © evgenyatamanenko—Fotolia.com
   49 © lassedesignen—Fotolia.com
   53 © Coloures-pic—Fotolia.com
   57 © kojihirano—Fotolia.com

表紙 © alphaspirit—Fotolia.com

はじめに

　本書は様々なトピックを中心に各ユニットが構成された全15ユニットのテキストです。トピックの内容は、「人権と防犯」「遺伝子医療と倫理」などの社会的に関心が深くなっている問題、「食料と資源」「グローバリゼーションと移民」などの国際社会が抱える問題、「実用教育と教養教育」などの教育に関する問題などを扱っています。「なぜ英語をやるのか」という英語教育の原点を考えさせるトピックもあります。

　本書の日本語のタイトルでは「クリティカルな思考」という言葉が使われていますが、英語のサブタイトルに使われている"Critical Thinking"とはどのようなことを言うのでしょうか。それは、書かれていることや言われたことをそのまま鵜呑みにするのではなく、「ちょっと待てよ」とよく考え、その内容を検証してみる思考のことです。私たちを囲む膨大な情報の信頼性や確実性を吟味するのにとても大切な思考法です。そうした思考法は、他人の言うことに惑わされることなく、学校や職場で人を客観的に評価することにも役立つことと思います。また、複雑に入り組んだ国際社会の問題についても賢明な判断をするのに身につけてほしい思考法です。

　クリティカルな思考の重要性は、他者を理解することを深くし、人、思想、文化などの差異を認めることにつながります。それは、どちらかが「善」でどちらかが「悪」、という二者択一的な思考から離れて、なぜ先方はそう考えるのだろうか、と「他者を理解しようとする」ことによって成り立つことなのです。それはまことのコミュニケーション能力に必要不可欠なものです。

　本書の本文の長さはいずれも350語前後になっています。じっくりと本文を読みその内容を整理したうえで検証することが出来ると思います。Exercisesには音声を利用したリスニング問題のほかに、学生のみなさんが自分自身で考え、自分の言葉を発信することを期待した問題がついています。

　本書が学生のみなさんのコミュニケーション能力の向上に役立つことが出来ればと願ってやみません。

2014年11月

James M. Vardaman

各ユニットの構成と使用法

各ユニットの冒頭の短い紹介文は本文のヒントにもなっています。

Warm-up
1. Pre-reading questions　本文に関連してくる質問が6問。
2. Pre-reading vocabulary　本文に出てくるやや難解な語のチェック。

Reading
- 350語前後からなる文章を読みます。
- パッセジの対向頁には学習者がメモや自分の考えを書き込むためのスペースを設けてあります。

Exercises
- Listening（計8問）　音声CD利用の正答選択問題が3問、T,F問題5問。
- 本文の内容について自分の考えなどをまとめたり、小グループに分かれて議論するための設問が合計6問ついています。授業の進捗状況等に合わせて柔軟に対応できます。
  3センテンス程度で本文のsummaryをつくる問題は英作文の練習にも応用できます。

CONTENTS

UNIT 1   **Who is following us?** 1
               誰かがついてくる？

UNIT 2   **Where does the corn go?** 5
               トウモロコシはどこへ行く？

UNIT 3   **Designer children?** 9
               個性の産み分けも可能に？

UNIT 4   **Troubled waters** 13
               枯渇する海の資源

UNIT 5   **A sore thumb in the neighborhood** 17
               個人の権利と公共性

UNIT 6   **Giving your heart to someone** 21
               命の重さ

UNIT 7   **Paying for good grades** 25
               アメとむち

UNIT 8   **Library and rental use of copyrighted materials** 29
               著作者は泣いている？

UNIT 9   **Judging and evaluating people** 33
               人を評価する基準の難しさ？

UNIT 10   **Limits to immigration** 37
               グローバリゼーションと移民問題

UNIT 11   **STEM or liberal arts?** 41
               実用教育と教養教育

UNIT 12   **Young children in day care** 45
               深刻な託児所不足

UNIT 13   **Affirmative action** 49
               援護か自立か

UNIT 14   **Why learn English?** 53
               なぜ英語をやるのか

UNIT 15   **Carbon offsets** 57
               環境か経済か

Unit 1

Who is following us?

誰かがついてくる？

社会のIT化が進むにつれ個人情報の流出やプライバシーの侵害が大きな問題となっている。防犯カメラについて言えば、こんなところにもと思うほど設置数も増えていて、個人の人権はどこまで守られるべきなのかも議論の的になっている。日常生活のなかで私たちの行動がカメラや最新のIT機器などによりどこまで捉えられているかを考察し、その功罪を考えてみよう。

▰▰▰▰▰▰▰▰▰▰▰▰▰▰ Warm-up ▰▰▰▰▰▰▰▰▰▰▰▰▰▰

1. Pre-reading questions

本文を読む前に考えよう。

(1) Is it justifiable to place cameras in public places?
(2) Who has the right to record people's movements?
(3) What are the advantages of security cameras?
(4) What are the disadvantages of security cameras?
(5) Who benefits from being observed?
(6) Whose rights are involved in observation?

2. Pre-reading vocabulary

本文に出てくる単語の意味を使用例を参考にして確認しよう。

prevent (l.3)	ex.: prevent automobile accidents	(	)
shoplifting (l.4)	ex.: be caught shoplifting	(	)
determine (l.9)	ex.: determine a plan of action	(	)
post (l.11)	ex.: post somebody abroad	(	)
install (l.15)	ex.: install new software	(	)
plan (l.16)	ex.: draw up a plan	(	)

Reading

Who is following us?

　　Everywhere we go, we are being watched. Security cameras record us in elevators, meeting rooms, hallways, restaurants, subway stations, and airports. These cameras are set up to protect people and prevent crimes. In stores, cameras are used to prevent shoplifting and to record attempts to steal money from the cashier.

　　Now those same cameras are serving another purpose: they are watching how we shop. They record how many people enter a store each hour it is open. Managers can use this data to create staff schedules. When crowds come, there will be enough salespeople to serve them. Cameras in one shop are able to determine customers' ethnicity. Noticing that groups of tourists from one foreign country came in the shop at the same time every day, the manager posted salespeople who could speak their language.

　　Cameras also observe what we look at and how we move through the store. Managers use this data to decide where to place items on shelves and how to attract the customer's attention. Some stores have installed wide-screen monitors to display floor plans and advertisements for special sale items. Behind the monitor is a camera which notes eye movement and uses a database to try to determine the viewer's gender and age group. On the basis of this data, the screen then changes to show advertisements for products that might appeal to the person looking at it.

　　Recently some stores are tracking signals from mobile phones. They can find out how many people walking by their store actually come in. They can count how long people stay in the store. Although they do not know who owns a phone, they do know how frequently a phone enters the store. In other words, they can recognize repeat customers. Shop managers find this information very helpful for their business.

Notes

1 **security camera**「防犯カメラ；監視カメラ」／7 **how we shop**「私たちがどのように買い物をするのか」／**each hour it is open**「店が開いている間の1時間ごとに」／10– **Noticing that..., the manager posted....** 分詞構文の用例。「…のことに気がついたので、店長は…を配置した」／20– **find out**「(答)を出す；発見する」

############################ *Exercises* ############################

I. Individual class activities

(1) CDから流れる質問を聴いて正しい答をそれぞれ選びなさい。

　1.
　　　a. in subway stations　　b. in schools　　c. in elevators

　2.
　　　a. to create staff schedules　　b. to decide when to open their shops
　　　c. to choose men or women as workers

　3.
　　　a. gender　　b. ethnicity　　c. height and weight

(2) CD を聴いてその内容が正しければ T を、間違っていれば F を丸で囲みなさい。

1. T　F　　2. T　F　　3. T　F　　4. T　F　　5. T　F

(3) 本文の要点を 3 センテンス程度にまとめなさい。

....

....

....

II. Small group activities

(1) 本文の重要なポイントについて議論しよう。

(2) 次の各文の内容を「正当と思う (pro)」、「不当と思う (con)」の立場になってその理由をいくつか明確に述べなさい。

1. Security cameras are used in public places (streets, stations, etc.).

Reasons why this *is* justifiable (pro):

(a)

(b)

(c)

Reasons why this is *not* justifiable (con):

(a)

(b)

(c)

2. Cameras and tracking devices are used in stores to monitor customers.

Reasons why this *is* justifiable (pro)

(a)

(b)

(c)

Reasons why this is *not* justifiable (con)

(a)

(b)

(c)

(3) グループ内の議論の中で提起された重要なポイントをまとめてみよう。

Unit 2

Where does the corn go?
トウモロコシはどこへ行く？

現代は農産物が食料としてではなくエネルギー資源としても使われる時代である。トウモロコシの大生産地のアメリカでは石油を補う重要なエネルギー資源としてのトウモロコシの利用はもはや国策にもなっている。環境にやさしいエネルギーとしての価値も高い一方で、農産物価格の高騰や食料不足などにもおおきな影響を与えるそうした利用法について考えてみよう。

||||||||||||||||||||||||||||| Warm-up |||||||||||||||||||||||||||||

1. Pre-reading questions
本文を読む前に考えよう。

(1) What are the possible sources of fuel?
(2) Should a country be dependent on imports for fuel?
(3) Which fuels are environmentally friendly?
(4) What crops are most common in Japan?
(5) Are those crops consumed locally?
(6) What weather events affect crop production?

2. Pre-reading vocabulary
本文に出てくる単語の意味を使用例を参考にして確認しよう。

breadbasket (l.1)	ex.: the region's breadbasket	( )
drought (l.3)	ex.: drought damages crops	( )
numerous (l.5)	ex.: make numerous changes	( )
portion (l.6)	ex.: a portion of food	( )
ferment (l.9)	ex.: fermented soybeans	( )
dependency (l.14)	ex.: be dependent on one's parents	( )
emissions (l.16)	ex.: reduce carbon dioxide emissions	( )

Reading

Where does the corn go?

America's Midwest has long been known as the "breadbasket" of the country. Enormous fields of sunflowers, wheat, oats, soybeans and corn stretch across the land. In the summer of 2012, however, the worst drought since 1956 hit the states of the Midwest. The impact on corn, the main crop, was of particular interest for numerous reasons.

A small portion of corn is eaten fresh, canned, or frozen. Corn meal is used in making corn bread. Another portion is used in the production of food and beverages, in the form of cornstarch and corn syrup. Corn syrup can even be fermented into grain alcohol that is used in distilling Bourbon whiskey. Another 13% of American's corn is sold abroad. Another third of American corn is used as feed for cows, pigs, and other animals. But the largest percentage, close to 40%, is used in the production of a fuel called ethanol.

On the surface, ethanol is environmentally friendly. Ethanol produced from corn reduces America's dependency on fossil fuels, such as coal, oil and natural gas. It also reduces dependency on oil imports from other nations. Further, ethanol helps to reduce global carbon dioxide emissions. Blended with gasoline, ethanol increases the overall supply of gasoline and lowers gasoline prices.

With the continued drought, from June to August, corn prices rose over 60%. As a result, consumers around the world would find prices of a wide variety of products rise.

The 2012 drought stimulated a debate over the appropriate use of corn supplies. According to federal law, in that year, 13.2 billion gallons of corn ethanol were set aside for blending with gasoline. That meant close to 40% of the annual corn crop. Opponents claimed that this was a misuse of corn. Rather than using such a large portion of corn for fuel, more should be set aside for food. If more corn were made available for people around the world, starvation could be reduced. The opponents of government policy claimed it was time to reconsider whether America's breadbasket should return to growing corn for food instead of fuel.

Notes

4– **was of particular interest for numerous reasons**「多くの理由で特別な関心ごとであった」／ 12 **ethanol** [éθənɔ́ːl]「エタノール」エチルアルコールと同じ。単にアルコールともいう。酒類の成分となるほかに燃料やさまざまな化学薬品の合成原料となる。／ 13 **on the surface**「うわべは」／ 25 **set aside for ...**「…のために取っておく」／ 25– **If more corn were made available for people**「もしもっと多くのトウモロコシが人びとの求めに応じられるように作られたら」

############################ *Exercises* ############################

I. Individual class activities

(1) CDから流れる質問を聴いて正しい答をそれぞれ選びなさい。

  1.
      a. corn   b. soybeans   c. sunflowers

  2.
      a. It is exported to other countries.
      b. It is used as feed for cows and other animals.
      c. It is processed into ethanol.

  3.
      a. Reduce carbon dioxide emissions.   b. Increase the supply of gasoline.
      c. Mix with natural gas.

(2) CDを聴いてその内容が正しければTを、間違っていればFを丸で囲みなさい。

1. T F   2. T F   3. T F   4. T F   5. T F

(3) 本文の要点を3センテンス程度にまとめなさい。

....

....

....

II. Small group activities

(1) 本文の重要なポイントについて議論しよう。

(2) 次の各文の内容を「正当と思う (pro)」、「不当と思う (con)」の立場になってその理由をいくつか明確に述べなさい。

1. Only a small portion of corn is eaten by human beings.

Reasons why this *is* justifiable (pro):

(a)

(b)

(c)

Reasons why this is *not* justifiable (con):

(a)

(b)

(c)

2. Production of ethanol from corn to increase fuel for cars and machines.

Reasons why this *is* justifiable (pro)

(a)

(b)

(c)

Reasons why this is *not* justifiable (con)

(a)

(b)

(c)

(3) グループ内の議論の中で提起された重要なポイントをまとめてみよう。

Unit 3

Designer children?
個性の産み分けも可能に？

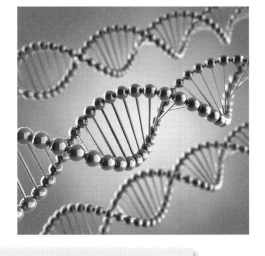

> iPS細胞(人工多能性幹細胞)から作った細胞を移植する世界初の手術が日本で2014年9月12日に目の難病治療に行われ、人工細胞の医療への応用が現実となってきた。再生医学や生殖医学、遺伝子工学などの分野でも科学の進歩はとどまるところを知らないようだが、そこから発生する倫理的な問題も現実味をおびてきている。

Warm-up

1. Pre-reading questions
本文を読む前に考えよう。

(1) How would you distinguish a "medicine" from a "drug"?
(2) Should a "health drink" be classified as medicine?
(3) What kinds of animals have been cloned so far?
(4) What are iPS cells and what can they do?
(5) Would you like to change any of your physical or mental abilities?
(6) Would you like to know your own chances of getting a disease?

2. Pre-reading vocabulary
本文に出てくる単語の意味を使用例を参考にして確認しよう。

synthetic (l.6)	ex.: made of synthetic material	( )
excel (l.8)	ex.: excel in writing	( )
enhance (l.9)	ex.: enhance a person's reputation	( )
injection (l.10)	ex.: get an injection	( )
regenerate (l.21)	ex.: regenerate a lost part of the body	( )
diabetes (l.23)	ex.: treat a person with diabetes	( )

Reading

Designer children?

Is there anyone who has not wanted to be a little bit stronger, faster, taller, or smarter?

Around the world, billions of dollars have been poured into research to produce drugs that will do these things. Drugs can help us gain muscle strength, stay focused, regain health, recover from injury, and either lose or gain weight. A synthetic version of the natural hormone EPO (erythropoietin) creates red blood cells, which boost endurance during long periods of activity. These products help people excel in bicycle races, foot races, baseball, football, and other sports.

But the desire to improve and enhance the natural body does not end with the use of supplements or injections of other substances. Research is also being carried on to select characteristics of the person before he or she is actually born. A significant step toward that goal was announced in 1997, when a sheep named Dolly gained great attention in the media. Dolly was the first mammal in history to be cloned from an adult animal cell. Immediately after the announcement that scientists had succeeded in cloning Dolly, the public began wondering, 'Would scientists one day be able to clone a human being?'

Cloning a human being seems virtually impossible. However, scientists are on the edge of making enormous progress through embryonic stem cell research. Dr. Shinya Yamanaka's work with induced pluripotent stem (iPS) cells has drawn special attention. Such research may help to isolate cells capable of becoming any tissue in the body. This might make it possible to regenerate organs of the human body for transplantation. Medical researchers also hope stem cell research will help them to cure illnesses like diabetes and injuries to the spinal cord. Others wonder whether such research could lead to genetic "enhancement": an improvement in muscle growth, memory development and increase in height. And could parents choose the gender of their child? Genetic engineering may soon make these possible.

Notes ───────

タイトル **designer children** 近未来に可能になるかもしれない、親の望みに合わせて遺伝子操作により生まれた子供。／6 **EPO** (erythropoietin)「エポ（エリスロポエチン）」赤血球の産生を促すホルモン。遺伝子組み換えによって作られた人工 EPO が貧血治療などにも用いられるが、持久力向上のためのドーピングとしても利用される。／13 **Dolly**「ドリー」1996 年 7 月にイギリスで誕生したクローン（遺伝的に同一である個体や細胞あるいは細胞の集合を指す生物学の用語）羊の名前。／14 **be cloned from ...**「…からクローンとして発生させられた」／19 **induced pluripotent stem (iPS) cells**「人工多能性幹細胞（iPS 細胞）」さまざまな組織や細胞になる可能性をもった細胞でほぼ無限に増える能力も持っている。山中教授は 2006 年にマウスの尻尾の細胞から、2007 年には人間の皮膚の細胞から作るのに成功した。／23 **spinal cord**「脊髄」

▰▰▰▰▰▰▰▰▰▰▰▰▰▰▰ Exercises ▰▰▰▰▰▰▰▰▰▰▰▰▰▰▰

I. Individual class activities

(1) CDから流れる質問を聴いて正しい答をそれぞれ選びなさい。

1.
    a. increasing physical strength   b. relaxing after long activity
    c. getting over an illness

2.
    a. Whether Dolly could be cloned again.
    b. Whether human beings could be cloned.
    c. Whether cloning was a dangerous process.

3.
    a. cure diabetes in humans.   b. create new organs for transplantation.
    c. clone a spinal cord.

(2) CDを聴いてその内容が正しければTを、間違っていればFを丸で囲みなさい。

1. T F   2. T F   3. T F   4. T F   5. T F

(3) 本文の要点を3センテンス程度にまとめなさい。

....

....

....

II. Small group activities

(1) 本文の重要なポイントについて議論しよう。

(2) 次の各文の内容を「正当と思う(pro)」、「不当と思う(con)」の立場になってその理由をいくつか明確に述べなさい。

   1. The use of drugs to enhance performance

   Reasons why the use of drugs *is* justifiable in some cases (pro):

   (a)

   (b)

   (c)

   Reasons why the use of drugs is *not* justifiable in some cases (con):

   (a)

   (b)

   (c)

   2. The use of iPS cells

   Reasons why their use *is* justifiable (pro)

   (a)

   (b)

   (c)

   Reasons why their use is *not* justifiable (con)

   (a)

   (b)

   (c)

(3) グループ内の議論の中で提起された重要なポイントをまとめてみよう。

Unit 4

Troubled waters
枯渇する海の資源

> 日本で大量消費されるマグロは世界の各国でも消費されるようになり資源保護のための漁獲制限が必要になってきた。海に面している国は排他的経済水域 (EEZ) で漁業資源を独占する権利が認められてはいる。しかし、世界の国々が獲り放題に魚を獲っていたら、マグロばかりでなく多くの漁業資源が枯渇しだすだろう。ウナギの養殖に使うシラスウナギの使用制限も必要になってきて食生活の嗜好の問題と資源との関わりなど考えるべきことは多い。

Warm-up

1. Pre-reading questions
本文を読む前に考えよう。

(1) Have you ever gone sport fishing?
(2) Who controls fishing on the beaches and shores of a country?
(3) What kinds of fish and marine animals live in the deep oceans?
(4) How can citizens help protect the oceans?
(5) Should there be limits to the amount of fish a country catches?
(6) What is an exclusive economic zone (EEZ)?

2. Pre-reading vocabulary
本文に出てくる単語の意味を使用例を参考にして確認しよう。

fishery (l.2)	ex.: a deep-sea fishery	( )
collapse (l.3)	ex.: the project collapsed	( )
reserve (l.8)	ex.: establish a marine nature reserve	( )
coastline (l.8)	ex.: an irregular coastline	( )
migrate (l.20)	ex.: salmon migrate to the sea	( )
compete (l.23)	ex.: compete to win a prize	( )

Reading

Troubled waters

The oceans are in trouble. Since 1900, certain species of fish have decreased in number by close to 90 percent. The cod fisheries off Canada's Atlantic Coast have come close to collapse. On the open seas, giant trawling ships from various nations suck up shrimp. Huge nets scrape the ocean floor, gathering every living thing. Half of the catch is thrown back into the sea, dead.

Meanwhile, close to one hundred thousand people a year travel to Leigh, New Zealand, a small farming and fishing community. They go there to visit the country's first marine reserve. When this small reserve on the coastline was established in 1977, conditions underwater were grim. A type of sea urchin, called kina, had eaten all of the kelp in the area and there were few fish or any other sea life. The cause was overfishing of snapper and spiny rock lobsters, which liked to eat the kina. When the snapper and lobster decreased, the kina rapidly increased.

When this marine reserve was created, things changed quickly. Snapper and lobsters were protected from humans. The lobsters and snappers quickly returned and they began eating the kina. The kelp returned, varieties of fish returned, and even fur seals returned.

At first, some of the community's fishermen opposed the creation of the reserve. Creating a marine reserve meant that they could not fish in that area. But now, the fishermen help protect the reserve, because it serves as a place for fish and lobster to reproduce. They then migrate out of the reserve into areas where fishermen can legally fish.

The deep seas, however, are under no one's effective control. Fleets of fishing ships compete to take economic advantage of the sea's resources, without concern that they might be overfishing. They catch many species of fish in huge nets, and simply throw away the ones that they do not plan to sell. While the New Zealand marine reserve cannot be a model for the oceans of the world, the whole world will suffer if some protective measures are not taken.

Notes

タイトル **troubled waters**「波立った水、（比ゆ的に）混乱」この意味の場合は必ず複数形で使う。／2 **by close to 90 percent**「殆ど9割方」 **off Canada's Atlantic Coast**「カナダの大西洋岸沖の」／3 **open sea(s)**「公海」各国の沿岸から12カイリ（約22キロ）までが領海、200カイリまでが排他的経済水域(EEZ)、公海はその外側の海域でどこの国の主権も及ばない。／4 **ocean floor**「海床」／6 **Leigh** [líː] ニュージーランド北部オークランド(Auckland)地方にあり住民は約400人。／9 **sea urchin**「ウニ」urchin「ハリネズミ」／10 **kina** [kíːnə] 食用ウニの1種。複数形も kina。 **kelp** コンブ科の大型褐藻類の総称。／11 **snapper** タイの1種。 **rock lobster(s)**「イセエビ」／16 **fur seal(s)**「オットセイ」seal アザラシ科の総称。／27 **measures** 通例複数形で「処置、手段」

Exercises

I. Individual class activities

(1) CDから流れる質問を聴いて正しい答をそれぞれ選びなさい。

1.
   a. cod fisheries
   b. tuna fisheries
   c. shrimp fisheries

2.
   a. They migrated to other areas.
   b. They became an important food for the community.
   c. They increased when lobsters decreased.

3.
   a. Some local fishermen were opposed to it.
   b. Fish stay only in the reserve and do not leave it.
   c. It is permitted to fish using a spear only.

(2) CDを聴いてその内容が正しければTを、間違っていればFを丸で囲みなさい。

1. T　F　　2. T　F　　3. T　F　　4. T　F　　5. T　F

(3) 本文の要点を3センテンス程度にまとめなさい。

II. Small group activities

(1) 本文の重要なポイントについて議論しよう。

(2) 次の各文の内容を「正当と思う (pro)」、「不当と思う (con)」の立場になってその理由をいくつか明確に述べなさい。

1. **Giant fishing fleets sail the oceans to take advantage of the sea's marine resources.**

    Reasons why they *are* justifiable (pro):

    (a)

    (b)

    (c)

    Reasons why they are *not* justifiable (con):

    (a)

    (b)

    (c)

2. **Fishing fleets should be given the right and the responsibility to determine the limits of their catches.**

    Reasons why this is justifiable (pro)

    (a)

    (b)

    (c)

    Reasons why this is not justifiable (con)

    (a)

    (b)

    (c)

(3) グループ内の議論の中で提起された重要なポイントをまとめてみよう。

Unit 5

A sore thumb in the neighborhood

個人の権利と公共性

景観を損ねたり近隣の陽当たりを悪くする建物が建設予定になると、地元の住民による「建設反対」の運動が起きる。近年では建築制限も細かくなってきているが、住宅地として利用できる土地面積の狭い日本の都市部のような地区での住民側の権利と建築する側の権利や新たに住民になる側の権利はどこまでお互いに守られるべきなのだろうか。

▮▮▮▮▮▮▮▮▮▮▮▮▮▮▮▮▮▮▮▮ Warm-up ▮▮▮▮▮▮▮▮▮▮▮▮▮▮▮▮▮▮▮▮

1. Pre-reading questions

本文を読む前に考えよう。

(1) Have you ever felt a house or building was "ugly"?
(2) Should certain kinds of businesses be banned near public schools?
(3) Are laws protecting the right to sunlight necessary?
(4) Why do neighborhoods of houses dislike tall condominium buildings?
(5) Is the "landscape" or "scenery" of a neighborhood decided by the residents?
(6) Should each house owner be free to choose the color of his or her house?

2. Pre-reading vocabulary

本文に出てくる単語の意味を使用例を参考にして確認しよう。

pedestrian (l.3)	ex.: cross a pedestrian bridge	( )
foundation (l.10)	ex.: build a strong foundation	( )
condominium (l.11)	ex.: buy a new condominium	( )
lawsuit (l.14)	ex.: bring a lawsuit against someone	( )
zoning (l.22)	ex.: oppose a zoning law	( )
unspoken (l.26)	ex.: an unspoken agreement	( )

Reading

A sore thumb in the neighborhood

The broad boulevard stretching from the south exit of Kunitachi station in western Tokyo is famous. Locally known as "University Boulevard", the road is wide, there are bike lanes, pedestrians have room to stroll, and it is lined with beautiful ginkgo and cherry trees. Sticking out like a sore thumb above the cherry trees on the west side of the boulevard is a tall condominium.

When planning for the building began, there were no zoning regulations concerning the height of buildings. When the building project was announced, the local government quickly passed a law that limited building height to 20 meters. When the new regulations came into effect in 2001, there was no structure on the building site. However, the digging of the foundations had begun. The developer therefore claimed that the condominium was already "under construction" before the law came into effect. The developer therefore claimed that the 40-meter building was legal.

Multiple lawsuits were filed against the developer for exceeding building height restrictions and for protection of the neighbors' interest in the "landscape". The issue continued through the court system for years. At least one court decision recognized the legally protected "right of landscape" and ordered that the top 20 meters of the building be removed.

In Kichijoji, a short train ride from Kunitachi, a different type of construction issue was taken up in the media. When manga artist Umezu Kazuo built a new house in a sedate neighborhood in Kichijoji, a neighborhood group protested loudly. The two-story house fit within the zoning regulations, so height was not at issue. The problem was that the appearance of the house did not fit the local tastes. It was painted in red-and-white stripes, which a group of residents claimed damaged the atmosphere of the neighborhood. The issue was one of subjective point of view and unspoken agreement among residents. In legal terms, it was a matter of individual choices and the rights of different property owners.

Notes

1 **Kunitachi station**「(JR 中央線) 国立駅」国立市は東京の中央部にあり、JR 国立駅から南へまっすぐ伸びる「大学通り」は幅が約 44 m ある。／3 **bike lanes**　bike=bicycle; motorcycle; motorbike ／4 **ginkgo** [gíŋkoʊ] 銀杏（ギンナン）。　**sticking out like a sore thumb**「目ざわりになる、場違いになる」／6 **regulation(s)**「条例、法規」traffic regulations「交通法規」／8 **local government**「地方自治体」この場合は国立市。／10 **building site**「建築用地」／14 **filed against ~ for …**　file against ~ for …「～に対して…を提起（提訴）する」／19 **Kichijoji**「吉祥寺」東京都武蔵野市の JR 吉祥寺駅を中心とする街。／20 **Umezu Kazuo**「楳図かずお」1936 年生まれ。恐怖漫画で著名。／21 **sedate** [sɪdéɪt] **neighborhood**「閑静な地区」／26 **in legal terms**　in ~ terms「～の面からみると、～の見地からみると」

▮▮▮▮▮▮▮▮▮▮▮▮▮▮▮▮▮▮▮ Exercises ▮▮▮▮▮▮▮▮▮▮▮▮▮▮▮▮▮▮▮▮▮

I. Individual class activities

(1) CDから流れる質問を聴いて正しい答をそれぞれ選びなさい。

1.

    a. It has lots of universities along it.

    b. Pedestrians have a lot of space to walk.

    c. There are trees along the sides of the road.

2.

    a. There was no building on the site when the law went into effect.

    b. The announcement of the regulations was in 2001.

    c. The building was being constructed when the new law was created.

3.

    a. The height of the house was different from other houses.

    b. The appearance of the house did not match the neighborhood.

    c. The two-story house was owned by a famous manga artist.

(2) CDを聴いてその内容が正しければTを、間違っていればFを丸で囲みなさい。

1. T　F　　　2. T　F　　　3. T　F　　　4. T　F　　　5. T　F

(3) 本文の要点を3センテンス程度にまとめなさい。

II. Small group activities

(1) 本文の重要なポイントについて議論しよう。

(2) 次の各文の内容を「正当と思う(pro)」、「不当と思う(con)」の立場になってその理由をいくつか明確に述べなさい。

1. **The Kunitachi lawsuits claimed that the height of the condominium destroyed the neighbor's rights to "landscape."**

    Reasons why the claims of the lawsuits *are* justifiable (pro):

    (a)

    (b)

    (c)

    Reasons why the claims of the lawsuits are *not* justifiable (con):

    (a)

    (b)

    (c)

2. **The neighbors in Kichijoji claimed that the individual property owner did not have the right to paint his house with red-and-white stripes, although he did not break any written regulations.**

    Reasons why the neighbors' claims *are* justifiable (pro)

    (a)

    (b)

    (c)

    Reasons why the neighbors' claims are *not* justifiable (con)

    (a)

    (b)

    (c)

(3) グループ内の議論の中で提起された重要なポイントをまとめてみよう。

Unit 6
Giving your heart to someone
命の重さ

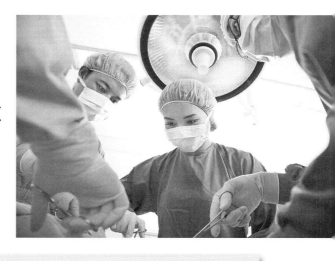

臓器の提供希望者はそれを必要としている患者の数に比べてまだ格段に少ないのが現状である。臓器移植に関しては提供者と患者との医学的適合性、それと手術までの時間などのほかにも問題がある。提供を受ける患者の優先順位はどのように決定されるのかなど臓器移植をめぐる問題について考えてみよう。

Warm-up

1. Pre-reading questions
本文を読む前に考えよう。

(1) Which human organs are most commonly transplanted?
(2) How is "death" determined by Japanese law?
(3) Are young people's lives more valuable than old people's lives?
(4) Should selling one's own organs be allowed?
(5) Who would you donate an organ to?
(6) Would you be willing to accept an organ from someone?

2. Pre-reading vocabulary
本文に出てくる単語の意味を使用例を参考にして確認しよう。

transplant (l.1)	ex.: a heart transplant operation	( )
illegal (l.3)	ex.: an illegal business	( )
donate (l.4)	ex.: donate money	( )
recipient (l.6)	ex.: the recipient of a prize	( )
available (l.9)	ex.: an available seat; become available	( )
criteria (l.16)	ex.: my criteria for judging music	( )
priority (l.18)	ex.: give priority to someone	( )

Reading

Giving your heart to someone

There is a limited supply of human organs for transplanting. Some organs from donors are not healthy. Some are not available at the right time for transplantation. Some cannot be transported to the hospital in time. In most countries, it is illegal to buy an organ, but it is possible to donate an organ to a family member.

Given the limited supply and the large need, various methods for selecting recipients have been proposed. One is to select recipients by a lottery, which would give each person an equal chance. A second is a system of "first come, first served." This is the system currently used in the U.S. Recipients are put on a waiting list in the area where they live. When an organ becomes available, it goes to the person on the waiting list who is closest and the sickest.

In setting priorities, should age be considered as a factor? In the U.S., preference is given to people under 18; they are the first considered to receive an organ by transplant. Over the age of 18, however, there is no preference by age. When an organ becomes available, it goes to the next recipient in line, regardless of how old he or she is.

Some people argue that other criteria should be used in selecting recipients. One argument is that a young person whose life is just beginning should have priority over an elderly person whose life is approaching an end.

Others argue that something we might call "social worth" should be taken into account. According to this argument, "potential benefit to society" is important. For example, a 30-year-old research scientist should have priority over a day laborer of the same age who did not finish high school. As another example, a mother of three young children should have priority over a single person of the same age.

Notes
5 **Given ~**「~とすれば」／ 7– **first come, first served** 諺。「先着順に応対、早い者勝ち」／ 10 **who is closest and the sickest**「もっとも近くにいてそして症状が重い（人）」／ 20 **potential benefit to society**「社会に対する潜在的な利益」／ 21– **day laborer**「日雇い労働者」

Exercises

I. Individual class activities

(1) CDから流れる質問を聴いて正しい答をそれぞれ選びなさい。

1.
   a. Human organs are always available.
   b. Timely transportation to hospitals is difficult.
   c. A family member can donate an organ.

2.
   a. The next person on the waiting list receives the organ.
   b. Recipients are chosen by a lottery.
   c. The person paying the most money receives the organ.

3.
   a. gender   b. educational background
   c. relations with parents

(2) CDを聴いてその内容が正しければTを、間違っていればFを丸で囲みなさい。

1. T　F　　　2. T　F　　　3. T　F　　　4. T　F　　　5. T　F

(3) 本文の要点を3センテンス程度にまとめなさい。

II. Small group activities

(1) 本文の重要なポイントについて議論しよう。

(2) 次の各文の内容を「正当と思う(pro)」、「不当と思う(con)」の立場になってその理由をいくつか明確に述べなさい。

1. **The donation of human organs should be decided by the individual only.**

    Reasons why this *is* justifiable (pro):

    (a)

    (b)

    (c)

    Reasons why this is *not* justifiable (con):

    (a)

    (b)

    (c)

2. **Priority in selecting recipients should be based only on age.**

    Reasons why this *is* justifiable (pro)

    (a)

    (b)

    (c)

    Reasons why this is *not* justifiable (con)

    (a)

    (b)

    (c)

(3) グループ内の議論の中で提起された重要なポイントをまとめてみよう。

Unit 7

Paying for good grades

アメとむち

勉強は自主的にやれれば言うことがないが、高校生ぐらいまでは遊びたいきもちの方が強いのがふつうであろう。「勉強しないと罰がある」より「勉強すればいいことがある」と思うことができれば勉強する身にも熱がはいるかもしれない。ましてその「いいこと」に金銭的なごほうびが含まれれば。

▰▰▰▰▰▰▰▰▰▰▰▰▰ Warm-up ▰▰▰▰▰▰▰▰▰▰▰▰▰

1. Pre-reading questions

本文を読む前に考えよう。

(1) Have you ever received a reward for good grades?
(2) Is a reward effective in encouraging a child to study?
(3) Have you ever been punished for getting a bad grade in school?
(4) Would you study harder if you could receive money for an "A"?
(5) What motivated you to study hard in high school?
(6) Is praise in words the best reward?

2. Pre-reading vocabulary

本文に出てくる単語の意味を使用例を参考にして確認しよう。

stubborn (l.1)	ex.: a stubborn old man	( )
dangle (l.4)	ex.: dangle a toy before a baby	( )
abandon (l.9)	ex.: abandon a plan	( )
motivate (l.12)	ex.: motivate Takashi to work hard	( )
deposit (l.16)	ex.: deposit money in the bank	( )
credit (l.22)	ex.: have a credit of ¥5,000 in a bank account	( )

Paying for good grades

　Imagine a man driving a wagon that is pulled by a mule, a rather stubborn animal. The man wants the mule to move forward, pulling the wagon. The man has two options for encouraging the mule. Either he can hit the mule on the behind with a stick, causing pain, or dangle a carrot just in front of the mule's face, offering a possible delicious reward for pulling the wagon.

　For centuries, parents and teachers have wondered whether the "stick approach" (punishment) or the "carrot approach" (reward) is the better way to get children to behave well and get good grades in school. Today most parents and teachers have abandoned the "stick" of physical punishment. Instead, they are using the "carrot" of reward. Researchers are trying to find out if rewards really work.

　Roland Fryer Jr., a professor at Harvard University, recently carried out an experiment in schools to see if paying students would motivate them. In four major American cities, Fryer's research project paid students for such behavior as attendance and good test scores. In a school in Chicago, ninth-graders were offered $50 for an A on a test, $35 for a B, and $20 for a C. They could earn up to $2000 a year. Half of the money was deposited into a bank account that they could use only after graduating from high school. In a school in Dallas, second-graders were offered $2 to read a book and answer a simple quiz about the book.

　Another group has taken a similar "carrot" approach. The Knowledge is Power Program (KIPP), a network of charter schools in the U.S., has offered "money" to students to arrive at school on time, participate in class and take a positive attitude. The "money" is actually credit that they can use to buy supplies at the school shop. The results of research so far do not prove whether students become better learners or whether they become smarter. Further, it would be ideal if children learn by themselves to be self-motivated and to love learning. In the short run, however, kids are happy to "earn as they learn."

Notes ─────

11 **Roland Fryer Jr.** 1977年生まれ。社会経済学、政治経済学を専門とする。30歳でアフリカ系アメリカ人として最も若くハーバード大学の専任教員となり現在教授。／ 11– **an experiment in schools** 後述の4つの都市（シカゴ、ダラス、ニューヨーク、ワシントン）の都市部200校以上の学校を対象にした教育方法の試みのこと。／ 12 **paying students** 「生徒に代価を支払う」／ 14 **ninth-graders** アメリカの公立学校はその地域を管轄する学校区の取り決めに従う。義務教育における学校制度は日本の6–3–3制と違って5–3–4制や6–2–4制が一般的であり、学年 (grade) の呼び方は 1st grade から 12th grade である。9th grade は high school の1年にあたる。なお、grade には成績（点）の意味もあるので注意。／ 19– **Knowledge is Power Program (KIPP), a network of charter schools** チャータースクールとはアメリカで教師・親・地域が州や学区の認可 (charter) を受けて設ける、公費によって運営される初等中等学校。KIPP（「知は力なりプログラム」）はそのなかのひとつで特にアフリカ系やヒスパニック系、低所得層の子供たちを対象に貧困からぬけ出すための学力向上を目標とする独自の教育プログラムを実行している。／ 25 **In the short run**「目先のことを考えれば、目先の計算では」Cf. in the long run.

############################ *Exercises* ############################

I. Individual class activities

(1) CDから流れる質問を聴いて正しい答をそれぞれ選びなさい。

1.
    a. Mules like carrots and will move forward in order to try to eat one.

    b. Carrots are healthy and mules choose to eat them.

    c. Mules are not fed well and will try to eat anything.

2.
    a. To see if students would participate in a survey

    b. To see how much students wanted to earn

    c. To see whether getting paid would motivate students to study

3.
    a. Students do not directly receive cash for what they do.

    b. Students are paid for each book they read.

    c. They receive money when they come to school.

(2) CDを聴いてその内容が正しければTを、間違っていればFを丸で囲みなさい。

1. T F   2. T F   3. T F   4. T F   5. T F

(3) 本文の要点を3センテンス程度にまとめなさい。

II. Small group activities

(1) 本文の重要なポイントについて議論しよう。

(2) 次の各文の内容を「正当と思う (pro)」、「不当と思う (con)」の立場になってその理由をいくつか明確に述べなさい。

   1. Giving children complete freedom to find their own motivation is essential.

   Reasons why this *is* justifiable (pro):

   (a)

   (b)

   (c)

   Reasons why this is *not* justifiable (con):

   (a)

   (b)

   (c)

   2. Physical rewards—such as cash or presents—should not be used to encourage students.

   Reasons why this *is* justifiable (pro)

   (a)

   (b)

   (c)

   Reasons why this is *not* justifiable (con)

   (a)

   (b)

   (c)

(3) グループ内の議論の中で提起された重要なポイントをまとめてみよう。

Unit 8

Library and rental use of copyrighted materials

著作者は泣いている？

印刷物に限らず何でも簡単にコピーできる時代になったが、「著作権」は「知的所有権」として保護されている。図書館の貸出し業務については著作権者側からすれば苦々しい問題かもしれないが、利用者側からすれば重宝で有難いことだと思う人が多いだろう。様ざまな著作者の権利について考えてみよう。

Warm-up

1. Pre-reading questions

本文を読む前に考えよう。

(1) How often do you purchase music and books?
(2) Have you ever copied a CD borrowed from a friend or a library?
(3) Do you regularly borrow materials from a library?
(4) What kind of materials do you copy on a copy machine?
(5) Do libraries pay for copyrighted materials?
(6) Will bookstores decline in the future?

2. Pre-reading vocabulary

本文に出てくる単語の意味を使用例を参考にして確認しよう。

publish (l.1)	ex.: publish a light novel	( )
blockbuster (l.3)	ex.: a blockbuster film	( )
income (l.7)	ex.: earn a large income	( )
secondhand (l.15)	ex.: a secondhand clothing shop	( )
profit (l.16)	ex.: make a profit	( )
enjoyment (l.19)	ex.: Music is my great enjoyment.	( )
purchase (l.21)	ex.: purchase a pair of shoes	( )
lend (l.23)	ex: lend someone a book	( )

Reading

Library and rental use of copyrighted materials

When a major writer such as Murakami Haruki publishes a new novel, hundreds of people line up at bookstores to buy a copy as soon as possible. When a blockbuster movie comes to a nearby theater, people rush to buy tickets online and fill the theaters. In these cases, the "buyer" or "consumer" pays money that supports the people who wrote, printed, and delivered the book and those who performed in, directed and produced the movie. The artists—and the other professionals who support their creative actions—depend on income from sales to support themselves and their families. Most of us would agree that they have a right to profit from the time and energy they put into creating these books and movies. Copyright laws protect the rights of writers, moviemakers, artists and video-game creators.

But how far and how long are those rights protected? It is clear that you cannot scan a copy of Murakami's latest bestseller, print it with your name as the author, and sell it in a bookstore. However, you can sell your copy of his book to a secondhand bookstore or to an online bookstore. Murakami makes no money from this. In fact, in a sense he may lose profit because a buyer is not buying a copy of his new book from a bookstore.

School libraries and public libraries provide a great service. They provide books and music CDs for our enjoyment without cost. Users sign up on waiting lists to borrow a particularly popular item and it may be months before their turn comes. The library makes a one-time purchase of these items, but the items may be used by dozens of people without charge. Certain holders of copyrights feel that they should be paid for this lending of the material they created. Is it time to reexamine the free lending of copyrighted materials by libraries?

Notes

4 **the "buyer" or "consumer"** 内容的にはどちらも購入者で、同じことを違った語で言っている。ここの consumer は映画などのサービスやソフトウェアなどのデジタルコンテンツの購入者のこと。反対語はそれぞれ seller と producer。／9 **the time and energy they put**「彼らが費やした時間とエネルギー」／19– **sign up on waiting list(s)**「待機者リストに登録する」／21 **make a one-time purchase**「1回だけの買い物をする」

############################ **Exercises** ############################

I. Individual class activities

(1) CDから流れる質問を聴いて正しい答をそれぞれ選びなさい。

1.
 a. creative actions   b. copyrights   c. rights to profit

2.
 a. To copy a novel, put your name on it, and sell it?
 b. To sell a music CD an online store.
 c. To sell a book you have bought to a secondhand store.

3.
 a. They lend materials for a small charge.
 b. They order books and CDs and pay for them.
 c. They never make people wait to borrow materials

(2) CDを聴いてその内容が正しければTを、間違っていればFを丸で囲みなさい。

1. T　F　　2. T　F　　3. T　F　　4. T　F　　5. T　F

(3) 本文の要点を3センテンス程度にまとめなさい。

....

....

....

II. Small group activities

(1) 本文の重要なポイントについて議論しよう。

(2) 次の各文の内容を「正当と思う(pro)」、「不当と思う(con)」の立場になってその理由をいくつか明確に述べなさい。

1. **Copyright laws cover only the first sale of a book or movie.**

    Reasons why this *is* justifiable (pro):

    (a)

    (b)

    (c)

    Reasons why this is *not* justifiable (con):

    (a)

    (b)

    (c)

2. **Public and school libraries should pay extra for lending copyrighted materials, including books and music CDs.**

    Reasons why this is justifiable (pro)

    (a)

    (b)

    (c)

    Reasons why this is not justifiable (con)

    (a)

    (b)

    (c)

(3) グループ内の議論の中で提起された重要なポイントをまとめてみよう。

Unit 9
Judging and evaluating people

人を評価する基準の難しさ？

スポーツでも陸上競技や水泳などのように記録によって優劣がはっきりしているものと審判の採点によって勝敗が決するものがある。主観が入る判定は論議の的になる。日本では入試や就職試験など人の一生に大きな影響を与える競争で公平無私な選別が行われているのだろうか考えてみよう。

Warm-up

1. Pre-reading questions
本文を読む前に考えよう。

(1) Do you think the Japanese university entrance exam system is fair?
(2) Are there any factors in the exam system that you would like to change?
(3) Do you think opening the gates to everyone would be a good idea?
(4) Are interviews necessary for entering university?
(5) How do Japanese companies choose new employees?
(6) Should a person's physical appearance be considered in choosing employees?

2. Pre-reading vocabulary
本文に出てくる単語の意味を使用例を参考にして確認しよう。

evaluate (l.1)	ex.: evaluate a student's ability	( )
virtually (l.4)	ex.: virtually impossible	( )
admission (l.8)	ex.: applicants for admission	( )
aptitude (l.13)	ex.: an aptitude for languages	( )
attach (l.18)	ex.: attach a photograph	( )
applicant (l.21)	ex.: interview job applicants	( )
determine (l.26)	ex.: determine the meaning of a word	( )

Reading

Judging and evaluating people

Athletes are evaluated according to how fast they run, how high they jump or how accurately they throw a ball. In the business world, competitors are evaluated according to how new their ideas are, how quickly they bring out new product models, how many they sell or how they gain market share. In virtually every part of our lives, we evaluate others and are evaluated by others. But are the criteria for evaluation fair?

Perhaps our first evaluation hurdles are entrance exams to schools. In Japan, admission to elite high schools and universities are, for the most part, determined by a once-a-year examination. Every applicant has an equal chance on that test. If you study very hard, you will be able to get into your first-choice university. American universities, by contrast, consider various factors, including your record in high school, volunteer activities, athletic participation, your scores on a national aptitude test—available several times a year—and sometimes a personal interview. Some American students might prefer the once-a-year exam because they could focus on preparing for just that.

The second evaluation hurdle is the hunt for a job. Japanese students looking for jobs following graduation stay up late at night filling in "entry sheets" and creating resumes with a recent photo attached. American students start looking for places to do internships in the summers even in their freshman year. Their resumes, also called CVs (curriculum vitae), usually do not require a photo or even the applicant's age. Employers are not supposed to give preference according to what someone looks like or how young or old they are. American students may put off looking for work until after they graduate.

Each school, university, employer and society has its own criteria for evaluating people. Whether these individual criteria are fair, useful and accurate is highly significant, not just for the individuals who want to participate but for determining the success or failure of that group. The setting of the criteria deserves serious consideration.

Notes ───────
5 **criteria** 単数形は criterion.「基準」／ 11 **by contrast**「それに対して」／ 12 **athletic participation**「運動競技への参加」スポーツ部で活動すること。／ 12– **national aptitude test— available several times a year** 全米で実施される大学進学適性試験 SAT (Scholastic Aptitude Test) や学習達成度測定試験 ACT (American College Test) のことで両方合わせて受験できる。／ 17 **following graduation** この場合の follwing は前置詞。／ 20 **resume(s)** resume [rɪzúːm]「履歴書」／ **curriculum vitae** [kəríkjʊləm váɪtə] vitae は vita の複数形。／ 22– **may put off looking for work**「仕事を探すのを延ばしてもさしつかえがない」

############################ **Exercises** ###########################

I. Individual class activities

(1) CDから流れる質問を聴いて正しい答をそれぞれ選びなさい。

1.
    a. They are used for athletes.   b. They evaluate applicants.
    c. They are held once a year.

2.
    a. They are easier to get into.   b. Various factors are considered.
    c. Students take one test per year.

3.
    a. They fill out lots of entry sheets.
    b. They look for internships to do in the summers.
    c. They get jobs before they graduate.

(2) CDを聴いてその内容が正しければTを、間違っていればFを丸で囲みなさい。

1. T　F　　　2. T　F　　　3. T　F　　　4. T　F　　　5. T　F

(3) 本文の要点を3センテンス程度にまとめなさい。

II. Small group activities

(1) 本文の重要なポイントについて議論しよう。

(2) 次の各文の内容を「正当と思う(pro)」、「不当と思う(con)」の立場になってその理由をいくつか明確に述べなさい。

1. **Admission to university should be based on academic ability evaluated by examinations.**

   Reasons why this *is* justifiable (pro):

   (a)

   (b)

   (c)

   Reasons why this is *not* justifiable (con):

   (a)

   (b)

   (c)

2. **Employers have the right to consider physical appearance in selecting employees.**

   Reasons why this *is* justifiable (pro)

   (a)

   (b)

   (c)

   Reasons why this is *not* justifiable (con)

   (a)

   (b)

   (c)

(3) グループ内の議論の中で提起された重要なポイントをまとめてみよう。

Unit 10

Limits to immigration
グローバリゼーションと移民問題

日本では少子化も影響して労働力不足が問題になっている。とりわけきつい仕事の労働力不足は深刻である。だからと言って外国人労働者の受け入れに日本が積極的ということはない。EU 諸国やアメリカなどの外国人労働者をめぐる現状はどのようで、どのような問題を抱えているのだろうか。

||||||||||||||||||||||||||| Warm-up |||||||||||||||||||||||||||

1. Pre-reading questions
本文を読む前に考えよう。

(1) Would you consider working outside of Japan?
(2) Where do you see workers from other countries in Japan?
(3) Why would foreign people want to work in Japan?
(4) What kinds of jobs do Japanese do in other countries?
(5) What problems to foreign workers face in other countries?
(6) Will Japan need more workers from abroad in the future?

2. Pre-reading vocabulary
本文に出てくる単語の意味を使用例を参考にして確認しよう。

reside (l.5)	ex: reside in Boston	( )
wealthy (l.9)	ex: become wealthy through buying stocks	( )
struggle (l.13)	ex: struggle for power	( )
burden (l.13)	ex: a burden on society	( )
demanding (l.16)	ex: a demanding job	( )
promotion (l.25)	ex: get a promotion	( )

Reading

Limits to immigration

There was a time when you had to stay where you were, even if you didn't like it. But now cheaper transportation, more sources of information, and easier communication makes packing up and moving more possible. That is why many Spanish-speaking people now live in southern California, many Arabic-speaking people now reside in France, and Russian speakers can be heard around the world.

While some people praise the trend toward "globalization," when it comes to immigration and working, the situation becomes more complex. Virtually every nation opens its gates to tourists and other short-term visitors, because tourists spend money and then go home. Some nations open their gates to wealthy immigrants and to those who promise to start businesses. But the gates are usually closed to low-skilled workers who would like to work full-time in that country. These countries fear that immigrants might take away jobs from citizens who are struggling to find work. They also fear that immigrants would place a burden on social services like schools and hospitals.

Like other nations, America has lots of certain kinds of job openings that even unemployed citizens are not eager to apply for. These jobs are dirty or demanding, so Americans avoid them. People in other countries would be happy to do even this unpleasant work—if they could get a working visa. Cleaning hotel rooms, washing dishes, and taking care of elderly people are among the openings that are available.

The U.S. government is considering creating a new visa program for low-skilled foreign workers. It would allow visiting workers to take year-round positions, not just seasonal agricultural jobs or temporary work. It would allow foreign workers to move from employer to employer, to earn the same wages as American workers, to have a chance at promotion, and to apply for permanent residency after a year. Eventually they could apply for U.S. citizenship.

Notes
2 **transportation**「運賃」不可算名詞。 **sources of information**「情報資料」／3 **communication**「交通連絡」不可算名詞。／6– **when it comes to ~**「~のことになると」／10 **promise to ~**「~の見込みがある」／13– **place a burden on social services**「社会事業の上に重い荷を置く」social services と複数形になると特に政府が行う社会事業を意味する。／15 **job openings**「仕事口、就職先」

############################ *Exercises* ############################

I. Individual class activities

(1) CDから流れる質問を聴いて正しい答をそれぞれ選びなさい。

  1.
      a. low-skilled workers   b. long-term visitors   c. tourists

  2.
      a. jobs that are hard to do   b. jobs that are rewarding
      c. jobs with chances of promotion

  3.
      a. workers only on farms   b. year-round workers
      c. seasonal workers only

(2) CDを聴いてその内容が正しければTを、間違っていればFを丸で囲みなさい。

1. T　F　　2. T　F　　3. T　F　　4. T　F　　5. T　F

(3) 本文の要点を3センテンス程度にまとめなさい。

II. Small group activities

(1) 本文の重要なポイントについて議論しよう。

(2) 次の各文の内容を「正当と思う (pro)」、「不当と思う (con)」の立場になってその理由をいくつか明確に述べなさい。

1. People should be free to live and work in any nation they choose.

Reasons why this *is* justifiable (pro):

(a)

(b)

(c)

Reasons why this is *not* justifiable (con):

(a)

(b)

(c)

2. Priority for jobs should be given to a country's own citizens, regardless of ability.

Reasons why this *is* justifiable (pro)

(a)

(b)

(c)

Reasons why this is *not* justifiable (con)

(a)

(b)

(c)

(3) グループ内の議論の中で提起された重要なポイントをまとめてみよう。

Unit 11

STEM or liberal arts?
実用教育と教養教育

大学にとにかく合格することだけが目標で、卒業後の進路を考えずに入学する人は理系と文系を問わずに多いのはなぜだろうか。また、大学教育は企業の求める人材を供給するのが目的なのだろうか。自分が大学で学びたいことは何なのか、再考してみる必要があるかもしれない。

Warm-up

1. Pre-reading questions
本文を読む前に考えよう。

(1) When you were a child, what did you want to become?
(2) In junior and senior high school, which subjects did you like?
(3) Which subjects did you avoid when it was possible?
(4) What is the purpose of university education?
(5) Is an education in "liberal arts" in decline?
(6) Should university prepare you for taking a job?

2. Pre-reading vocabulary
本文に出てくる単語の意味を使用例を参考にして確認しよう。

avoid (l.6)	ex.: avoid dangerous roads	( )
fill in (l.12)	ex.: fill in an application	( )
unfilled (l.15)	ex.: unfilled stadium seats	( )
stand for (l.15)	ex.: U.K. stands for the United Kingdom	( )
qualified (l.17)	ex.: a qualified doctor	( )
solid (l.19)	ex.: a solid musician	( )
potential (l.25)	ex.: a potential candidate for president	( )

STEM or liberal arts?

Across the globe, there seems to be a mismatch between the jobs that people are seeking and the jobs that companies actually offer. The result is that job-hunters cannot find work and businesses cannot find employees.

Parents and teachers have long told children, "Follow your dreams." So, students focus first on getting into the next level of schooling and second on doing what is interesting. Along the way, they usually do their best to avoid the "hard" subjects in school, unless those subjects are on the entrance exams. Once they get into university, they are somewhat lost because they have accomplished their "goal" of passing the entrance exam, but do not have a clear idea of what to do during the next four years. As the third year comes around, they once again try to "follow their dreams" by looking for jobs in extremely competitive companies. They fill in dozens of "entry sheets" and wait for a call from the company to come for an interview. That phone call rarely comes.

There are jobs, however, in small and medium-size companies. There are also jobs in the STEM fields that go unfilled. STEM stands for Science, Technology, Engineering and Math. Efforts are being made to encourage interest in these fields beginning in elementary school so that there will be qualified candidates for jobs after graduation from universities. The job-seekers in these fields will be successful and the companies will be able to hire employees with a solid background.

But is the ultimate goal of university education to provide employees? Many would contend that university years should be devoted to broadening one's vision of the world. Time should be spent in reexamining Japanese history or reading and thinking deeply about what makes Natsume Soseki's *Kokoro* a classic work of modern literature. In other words, four years should focus on liberal arts, developing the student as an individual who can think for himself, not as a potential employee.

Notes

タイトル **STEM** 本文の 15 行目を参照のこと。　**Liberal arts** 専門科目に対して、一般的な知識を与え、自分で考える力などの知力の発展を目的とした語学、文学、哲学、歴史、自然科学などを言う。／1 **across the globe**「地球横断的に」／3 **businesses** > business　ここでは「企業」の意味。／5 **students focus first on getting into the next level of schooling**「生徒たちは第一に次の段階の学校（教育）に入ることに関心を集中する」schooling［名詞］「学校教育（を受けること）」／6 **along the way**「途中で」／8 **are somewhat lost**　be lost「自分を見失う；混乱する」／15 **go unfilled**「満たされていない状態である」

////////////////////////////// *Exercises* //////////////////////////////

I. Individual class activities

(1) CDから流れる質問を聴いて正しい答をそれぞれ選びなさい。

　1.
　　a. Good advice.　　　　　　b. Advice that adults often give.
　　c. The worst advice possible.

　2.
　　a. Engineering　　　b. Medicine　　　c. Science

　3.
　　a. There aren't many of them.　　b. They are highly competitive.
　　c. They want to hire solid job-seekers.

(2) CD を聴いてその内容が正しければ T を、間違っていれば F を丸で囲みなさい。

1. T F   2. T F   3. T F   4. T F   5. T F

(3) 本文の要点を 3 センテンス程度にまとめなさい。

....

....

....

II. Small group activities

(1) 本文の重要なポイントについて議論しよう。

(2) 次の各文の内容を「正当と思う (pro)」、「不当と思う (con)」の立場になってその理由をいくつか明確に述べなさい。

1. **Students should choose a career early in life.**

   Reasons why this *is* justifiable (pro):

   (a)

   (b)

   (c)

   Reasons why this is *not* justifiable (con):

   (a)

   (b)

   (c)

2. **University education should be independent of considerations of future employment.**

   Reasons why this *is* justifiable (pro)

   (a)

   (b)

   (c)

   Reasons why this is *not* justifiable (con)

   (a)

   (b)

   (c)

(3) グループ内の議論の中で提起された重要なポイントをまとめてみよう。

Unit 12

Young children in day care

深刻な託児所不足

女性の社会進出は近年目覚ましいものがあるというもののまだまだ職場でも家庭でも男女平等とはいっていないだろう。働く女性が母親になるとまず直面するのが保育園などの適切な託児所の不足である。子供を持つ女性が直面する深刻な問題について考えてみよう。

Warm-up

1. Pre-reading questions

本文を読む前に考えよう。

(1) Is it important to have women in Japan's workforce?
(2) Should mothers and fathers be able to take "childcare leaves*" from work?
(3) Should the government be responsible for operating childcare centers?
(4) Should there be a minimum age for nursery school kids?
(5) What hours do current nursery schools operate?
(6) Should all parents be charged the same fees for child care centers?

*childcare leave「育児休暇」

2. Pre-reading vocabulary

本文に出てくる単語の意味を使用例を参考にして確認しよう。

CEO = Chief Executive Officer (l.1)	ex.: the CEO of Microsoft	( )
corporation (l.4)	ex.: work for a major corporation	( )
subsidize (l.15)	ex.: subsidize education	( )
private (l.21)	ex.: go to a private university	( )
surrender (l.22)	ex.: surrender one's place in line	( )
portion (l.23)	ex.: eat a portion of …	( )

Reading

Young children in day care

It is big news when a woman becomes the CEO of any major company. But when Marissa Mayer was named CEO of Yahoo, there was another topic in the headlines: she was six months pregnant when she took the job. Many people wondered how she could run a major corporation and take care of a newborn child at the same time. Her solution was to build a nursery, in a room next to her office, out of her own pocket. She—with her baby—returned to work two weeks after giving birth.

Not every woman, especially in Japan, can hold onto a job and take care of children at the same time. A generation ago, Japanese women tended to take dead-end jobs as a so-called "office lady" and worked until the first child came. Japanese women now, whether they are in management or not, often want to keep working even after having children. In many cases, they have to work to help support their families. But it is not easy. Married couples often live apart from their own parents, so there are no family members close by to offer help during the day. The Japanese government subsidizes day care centers for working families, but there are not enough centers in some areas. Tokyo's Setagaya ward has one of the longest waiting lists in the country.

Once a woman has survived the stressful job-hunting process and learned how to do her job, she faces "*hokatsu*," a new word for the competition for a place in a day care center for her child.

If she cannot find a slot in a public or private day care center, she may be forced to surrender her hard-earned job. If she has to depend on a private day care center, the cost may take a major portion of her salary.

Not everyone supports the idea of working mothers. Some feel that mothers should stay at home and raise their children. These people feel that leaving children all day in a day care center is bad for the development of the children.

Notes

2 **Marissa Mayer**「マリッサ・メイヤー」元 Google 社副社長で 2012 年 7 月に米 Yahoo! の CEO に就任した。／5 **build a nursery, in a room next to her office**「育児室を設ける、それも彼女のオフィスの隣の部屋に」／7 **giving birth** < give birth「出産する」／8 **hold onto ~** = hold on to ~「~を手放さない」／11 **in management**「管理職にある」／14 **close by**「すぐそばに」／19 **"hokatsu,"**『保活』親が保育園を求めて一生懸命活動することを言った「就活」や「婚活」と同様な最近の造語。／21 **find a slot**「空きを見つける」／22 **hard-earned**「骨折って手に入れた」

▰▰▰▰▰▰▰▰▰▰▰▰▰▰▰▰▰ Exercises ▰▰▰▰▰▰▰▰▰▰▰▰▰▰▰▰▰

I. Individual class activities

(1) CDから流れる質問を聴いて正しい答をそれぞれ選びなさい。

1.
    a. She became a CEO.   b. She stopped working at Yahoo.
    c. She became a mother.

2.
    a. The government gives financial support to public day care centers.
    b. Private day care centers receive government support.
    c. Women tend to work at day care centers when they become mothers.

3.
    a. Public day care centers are hard to get into.
    b. Private day care centers are better than public ones.
    c. Working mothers cannot make use of these centers.

(2) CDを聴いてその内容が正しければTを、間違っていればFを丸で囲みなさい。

1. T　F　　2. T　F　　3. T　F　　4. T　F　　5. T　F

(3) 本文の要点を3センテンス程度にまとめなさい。

II. Small group activities

(1) 本文の重要なポイントについて議論しよう。

(2) 次の各文の内容を「正当と思う(pro)」、「不当と思う(con)」の立場になってその理由をいくつか明確に述べなさい。

1. **The primary responsibility of a mother should be childcare, not a career.**
   Reasons why this *is* justifiable (pro):
   (a)
   (b)
   (c)
   Reasons why this is *not* justifiable (con):
   (a)
   (b)
   (c)

2. **Providing child care centers is the responsibility of the government.**
   Reasons why this *is* justifiable (pro)
   (a)
   (b)
   (c)
   Reasons why this is *not* justifiable (con)
   (a)
   (b)
   (c)

(3) グループ内の議論の中で提起された重要なポイントをまとめてみよう。

Unit 13

Affirmative action

援護か自立か

アメリカでは人種や性に関わる格差に対応する措置として affirmative action（差別是正積極的措置）という、歴史的に差別を受けた人たちに優先的な機会を与える措置がある。そうした措置はまだ必要か、あるいは時代遅れか、それとも逆差別なのか。

Warm-up

1. Pre-reading questions

本文を読む前に考えよう。

(1) Does Japan have laws that protect certain groups of citizens?
(2) Do Japanese universities offer equal chances to all applicants?
(3) Is "affirmative action" necessary in Japan?
(4) When did slavery begin in America?
(5) In America are blacks treated equally as whites?
(6) Does society have a duty to help certain groups?

2. Pre-reading vocabulary

本文に出てくる単語の意味を使用例を参考にして確認しよう。

discriminate (l.1)	ex.: discriminate against women	( )
affirmative (l.7)	ex.: an affirmative action	( )
minority (l.12)	ex.: belong to an ethnic minority	( )
dependency (l.22)	ex.: dependency on one's parents	( )
abolish (l.27)	ex.: abolish a law	( )
legislature (l.29)	ex.: elect a member of the legislature	( )
eliminate (l.30)	ex.: eliminate risks	( )

Reading

Affirmative action

African Americans have always been discriminated against. Over 400 years, millions of people were taken from Africa and made to work as slaves in America and other countries. Legally, all black slaves were freed in 1863. For the first time, they became citizens of the U.S. But a century later, black people were still being discriminated against in schools, companies and society as a whole. Dr. Martin Luther King's "I Have a Dream" speech in 1963 called for equality of opportunity for all people. As a result of the Civil Rights Movement (1954–1968), "affirmative action" was an active effort to provide equal opportunities to African Americans in education and employment. This effort also applied to women, members of other minority groups, and people with physical and mental disadvantages.

The U.S. government passed "affirmative action" laws that affected different parts of society. One type of law made it easier for blacks and other minorities to enter universities. Quotas and percentages were established, which gave opportunities to certain kinds of applicants. Another type of law required companies to have a percentage of minority employees. This changed hiring practices and promotion practices. A third type of law gave special treatment to members of minorities wanting to start businesses, by guaranteeing loans from banks to start companies.

Today, a half century after Dr. King's speech, affirmative action is being debated. Opponents of affirmative action say that discrimination has disappeared. They say that everyone is now equal and the time for giving special treatment to certain people is now over. They point out that America even has a black president. They also say that giving special treatment creates dependency on government rather than creating personal independence.

Supporters of affirmative action say that even though some progress has been made, discrimination still exists. They say that disadvantaged people still need affirmative action laws to protect them and guarantee they have equal opportunities. If these laws are abolished, they claim, prejudice and discrimination will grow worse.

This debate is ongoing in books, the media, state legislatures, Congress and the U.S. Supreme Court. Whether the laws are eliminated, kept or strengthened will affect Americans of all types.

Notes

1 **African American(s)** African American はアフリカ系アメリカ人をいう時の中立的な語として現在一般的に用いられている。／5– **Dr. Martin Luther King** (1929–68) 牧師。非暴力の抵抗による人種差別撤廃を訴えた公民権運動 (Civil Rights Movement) の指導者。1964年ノーベル平和賞受賞。1968年暗殺される。／13 **quota(s)**「(受け入れる)割り当て数」／16 **practice(s)**「(これまでの)やり方、慣行」／23 **independence**「自立心」

////////////////////////////// **Exercises** //////////////////////////////

I. Individual class activities

(1) CDから流れる質問を聴いて正しい答をそれぞれ選びなさい。

1.

    a. Millions of Africans were made to work in America

    b. All slaves in America were legally freed.

    c. Black people were no longer discriminated against.

2.

    a. Blacks were given special advantages to enter universities.

    b. Black businesses were assisted by loans.

    c. Blacks were given the right to vote.

3.

    a. It has grown worse.   b. It still continues.   c. It has disappeared.

(2) CDを聴いてその内容が正しければTを、間違っていればFを丸で囲みなさい。

1. T　F　　2. T　F　　3. T　F　　4. T　F　　5. T　F

(3) 本文の要点を3センテンス程度にまとめなさい。

II. Small group activities

(1) 本文の重要なポイントについて議論しよう。

(2) 次の各文の内容を「正当と思う (pro)」、「不当と思う (con)」の立場になってその理由をいくつか明確に述べなさい。

1. Affirmative action has accomplished major changes in American society.

Reasons why this *is* justifiable (pro):

(a)

(b)

(c)

Reasons why this is *not* justifiable (con):

(a)

(b)

(c)

2. Affirmative action programs are still necessary in America.

Reasons why this *is* justifiable (pro)

(a)

(b)

(c)

Reasons why this is *not* justifiable (con)

(a)

(b)

(c)

(3) グループ内の議論の中で提起された重要なポイントをまとめてみよう。

Unit 14

Why learn English?
なぜ英語をやるのか

2011年に始まった小学校5年生からの英語教育も近い将来に3年生からに前倒しになる模様である。「英語を使える日本人の育成」、「アジアトップクラスの英語力の育成」など聞こえてくるかけ声は勇ましい。ここで「なぜ英語をやるのか」という根元的な問いに戻って考えるのも無意味ではなさそうだ。

||||||||||||||||||||||||||| Warm-up |||||||||||||||||||||||||||

1. Pre-reading questions

本文を読む前に考えよう。

(1) Which languages are the most useful for tourists?
(2) How do you feel about learning English?
(3) What is difficult about learning English?
(4) Do you think English should be a subject on entrance examinations?
(5) Is English necessary in your daily life?
(6) Do you think English ability will be essential in Japanese businesses in the future?

2. Pre-reading vocabulary

本文に出てくる単語の意味を使用例を参考にして確認しよう。

employment (l.4)	ex.: a candidate for employment	( )
negotiate (l.4)	ex.: negotiate a deal with a company	( )
exclusively (l.12)	ex.: books used exclusively in universities	( )
considerable (l.18)	ex.: a considerable number of spectators	( )
proficiency (l.18)	ex.: proficiency in French	( )
troublesome (l.18)	ex.: a troublesome situation	( )
capable of (l.22)	ex.: a person capable of judging art	( )
rewarding (l.25)	ex.: a rewarding experience	( )

Reading

Why learn English?

The average Japanese will tell you, "I'd like to be able to speak everyday English." It would be convenient for giving directions to foreign visitors on street corners in Japan. It would be helpful during a trip abroad. It would help in finding employment and in negotiating with overseas companies.

Until recently, young Japanese have studied English over a period of at least six years in junior and senior high school. What is the purpose of doing that? Fundamentally, it is to pass the exams to the next level of schooling. What is learned is a combination of "school English" (*gakko Eigo*) and "exam English" (*juken Eigo*). From this point of view, English is a "subject" not a "tool of communication."

When "oral communication" was introduced to the schools, this changed. But still, English is a tool that is used almost exclusively in the classroom. Once a student steps outside the school door, there is little use for English in communicating with others.

Recently companies like Uniqlo and Rakuten have made English their "in-house language" of communication. Other companies have pressed employees to take TOEIC and reach a specific score. As a result, employees are now spending considerable time and effort to achieve some proficiency in this troublesome foreign language.

Japanese society as a whole seems to think that learning English is a part of remaining globally competitive in the future. But does that mean that every Japanese person has to become capable of using English? Is it possible that only 10% of Japanese really need English and the other 90% don't need it? Communicating with people from foreign countries who cannot understand Japanese can be greatly rewarding, so that is one reason for learning English. Casual conversational English may be helpful during a ten-day trip abroad, but how often do most people go abroad? In sum, it is important for Japanese to consider more deeply why they "need to" learn English. If they really do need to use English, how much effort does it realistically take and is it worth the effort?

Notes
1 **The average Japanese will tell you** ここの will は特性や傾向を表す場合の用法。you はとくに訳さなくてよい一般的な「人」。／ 15 **Recently companies like Uniqlo and Rakuten … of communication.** ユニクロは2012年3月から、楽天は2012年7月から社内の公用語を英語にした。その他、日産やシャープなどの企業も社内の公用語を英語にしている。／ 20 **as a whole**「全体として」／ 27 **in sum**「要は、要するに」

############################## *Exercises* ##############################

I. Individual class activities

(1) CDから流れる質問を聴いて正しい答をそれぞれ選びなさい。

1.
    a. It is not necessary.   b. It is helpful.

    c. It is essential for everyone.

2.
    a. a subject   b. a tool   c. a goal

3.
    a. To become as proficient as possible.

    b. To use it in the workplace.

    c. To think about whether it is necessary.

(2) CDを聴いてその内容が正しければTを、間違っていればFを丸で囲みなさい。

1. T　F　　　2. T　F　　　3. T　F　　　4. T　F　　　5. T　F

(3) 本文の要点を3センテンス程度にまとめなさい。

....

....

....

II. Small group activities

(1) 本文の重要なポイントについて議論しよう。

(2) 次の各文の内容を「正当と思う(pro)」、「不当と思う(con)」の立場になってその理由をいくつか明確に述べなさい。

1. English ability is essential for global competitiveness.

Reasons why this *is* justifiable (pro):

(a)

(b)

(c)

Reasons why this is *not* justifiable (con):

(a)

(b)

(c)

2. Japanese do not need to study English in schools.

Reasons why this *is* justifiable (pro)

(a)

(b)

(c)

Reasons why this is *not* justifiable (con)

(a)

(b)

(c)

(3) グループ内の議論の中で提起された重要なポイントをまとめてみよう。

Unit 15
Carbon offsets
環境か経済か

1960年代から「環境問題」に対する意識は国によって低かったり、高かったりして差があった。今では、産業の環境に与える影響が国の境を超えていわゆるグローバルな問題となっている。「環境を守るか、経済発展を優先するか」世界が直面する問題である。

Warm-up

1. Pre-reading questions
本文を読む前に考えよう。

(1) Are you concerned about Japan's environment today?
(2) What are the main causes of air pollution?
(3) Do you recycle newspapers, bottles and cans at home?
(4) What types of transportation produce less pollution?
(5) How does pollution directly affect human beings?
(6) How can you directly reduce pollution?

2. Pre-reading vocabulary
本文に出てくる単語の意味を使用例を参考にして確認しよう。

reckless (l.4)	ex.: an accident caused by reckless driving	( )
treatment (l.4)	ex.: successful medical treatment	( )
emissions (l.10)	ex.: emissions standards	( )
carbon dioxide (l.11)	ex.: absorb carbon dioxide	( )
compensate (l.13)	ex.: compensate for a loss	( )
impose (l.18)	ex.: impose strict conditions	( )
absorb (l.27)	ex.: absorb ideas	( )

Reading

Carbon offsets

Until about the 1960s, most nations of the world were so concentrated on building their industries and economies that they did not think about the environment very often. A few voices, such as Rachel Carson in *Silent Spring*, warned about such reckless treatment of the natural world, but most people were more concerned with "progress" and GDP.

Gradually, however, people came to realize that clean air, clean drinking water, and clean soil are important for human health and survival. They became concerned about eliminating pollution, recycling resources, developing renewable energy, and preventing further damage to the planet. Once people learned about the dangers of greenhouse gases, they began to talk about ways to reduce emissions of carbon dioxide.

The Kyoto Protocol brought out the idea of a "carbon offset" as a way to make people aware of the problem and take action to compensate for the creation of carbon dioxide.

There is a general gap, however, between the so-called "developed countries" and "developing countries" when it comes to such environmental issues. The former became rich by creating CO_2 and damaging the environment. Now that they realize their mistakes, it seems as if they want to impose restrictions that would affect the economies of other countries. Restrictions on the use of fossil fuels, natural resources, and industrial growth would slow down the growth of the developing countries. The latter, in general, want to grow and have what the developed countries already have. What right do the wealthy countries have to tell the less-wealthy countries what to do? It would seem as if the developed countries are using "carbon emissions" and "environmental issues" to prevent the developing countries from progressing.

Another issue is whether "carbon offsets" actually work. One example is the planting of trees to absorb carbon dioxide. The problem is it is difficult to guarantee that the forest will survive. It may be burned—releasing more CO_2—or harvested for lumber. It might share the fate of a project sponsored by the British band Coldplay: it became a grove of dead mango trees.

Notes ───────
タイトル **carbon offset**「カーボンオフセット（温室効果ガス排出量相殺）」後述の「京都議定書」に参加する国々は国内での削減対策と同時に、温室効果ガスの吸収源として森林や農地で吸収される炭素をカウントすることが認められている。また、削減目標が達成できない国が排出量に余裕のある国から排出権を買い取る取引も認めている。／3 **Rachel Carson in *Silent Spring*** レイチェル・カーソンはアメリカの海洋生物学者・科学評論家 (1907–64)。鳥も歌わない春が来る、と農薬・化学薬品の危険を広く知らせた『沈黙の春』は1962年に出版された。／8– **renewable energy**「再生可能エネルギー」太陽光・風力・水力など。／10 **greenhouse gas(es)**「温室効果

ガス」二酸化炭素、メタン、フロンなど地球温暖化をもたらすガス。／ 12 **Kyoto Protocol**「京都議定書」1997 年に京都で開かれた、温暖化防止のための第 3 回目の国連気候変動枠組条約の締約国会議 (COP3:Conference of Parties) で採択された国際条約。この条約で、先進国全体で温室効果ガスを 2008 年から 2012 年の間に、1990 年比で約 5％削減することが義務付けられた。日本は 6％、後（2001 年）に京都議定書を離脱するアメリカは 7％、EU は 8％の削減を約束した。削減目標を達成できなかった国にはペナルティが適用されることになっている。一方、途上国には削減義務を求めていない。／ 19– **fossil** [fάsl] **fuel(s)**「化石燃料」石油、石炭、天然ガスなど。／ 24 **carbon emissions**［複数形］「（車、工場などから排出される二酸化炭素と一酸化炭素の）炭素排出物」／ 29– **It might share the fate … a grove of dead mango trees.**「コールドプレイ」は 2000 年代の最も成功したバンドのひとつといわれ、社会的・政治的運動にも積極的にかかわっている。しかし、彼らがカーボンオフセットの一端として、2002 年インドに植えたマンゴーの木 1 万本は 4、5 年で総て枯れてしまった。

|||||||||||||||||||||||||||||Exercises|||||||||||||||||||||||||||

I. Individual class activities

(1) CD から流れる質問を聴いて正しい答をそれぞれ選びなさい。

1.
   a. Rachel Carson   b. Kyoto Protocol   c. Developing countries

2.
   a. automobiles   b. greenhouse gases   c. environmental issues

3.
   a. They recycle carbon dioxide.   b. They release carbon dioxide.
   c. They absorb carbon dioxide.

(2) CD を聴いてその内容が正しければ T を、間違っていれば F を丸で囲みなさい。

1. T F   2. T F   3. T F   4. T F   5. T F

(3) 本文の要点を 3 センテンス程度にまとめなさい。

II. Small group activities

(1) 本文の重要なポイントについて議論しよう。

(2) 次の各文の内容を「正当と思う (pro)」、「不当と思う (con)」の立場になってその理由をいくつか明確に述べなさい。

1. **Restrictions on the use of fossil fuels should be placed on "developing countries."**

    Reasons why this *is* justifiable (pro):

    (a)

    (b)

    (c)

    Reasons why this is *not* justifiable (con):

    (a)

    (b)

    (c)

2. **There is no way to reduce emissions that is fair to all nations.**

    Reasons why this *is* justifiable (pro)

    (a)

    (b)

    (c)

    Reasons why this is *not* justifiable (con)

    (a)

    (b)

    (c)

(3) グループ内の議論の中で提起された重要なポイントをまとめてみよう。

You Make the Decision
Fifteen Topics for Critical Thinking
〈クリティカルな思考を養うための15章〉

編著者	James M. Vardaman
発行者	山 口 隆 史

発 行 所　　㈱ 音羽書房鶴見書店

〒113-0033　東京都文京区本郷 4-1-14
TEL 03-3814-0491
FAX 03-3814-9250
URL: http://www.otowatsurumi.com
e-mail: info@otowatsurumi.com

2015年 3 月 1 日　　初版発行
2015年 4 月 1 日　　 2 刷発行

組版・装幀　ほんのしろ
印刷・製本　㈱シナノ
■ 落丁・乱丁本はお取り替えいたします。